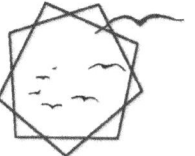

Northern

Compass

Northern Compass

ISOBEL CUNNINGHAM

Northern Compass
Copyright ©2015 Isobel Cunningham

ISBN: 978-1-940769-45-5
Publisher: Mercury HeartLink
Printed in the United States of America

Front cover photo: Patrick Martineau
http://pphoto.gallery/

All rights reserved. This book, or sections of this book, may not be reproduced or transmitted in any form without permission from the author, except for brief quotations embodied in articles, reviews, or used for scholarly purposes.

Permission is granted to educators to create copies of individual poems, with proper credits, for classroom or workshop assignments.

Contact the author at:
isobelmtl@yahoo.com

Mercury HeartLink
www.heartlink.com

Contents

ACKNOWLEDGMENTS	XI
DEDICATION	XIII

MONTREAL

Seduction	3
Don't Look for Logic Here	4
Montreal Pantoum I	6
Painters's Sky	7
Path to Morning	8
Cold Bronze	9
Tired Love	10
Hard Spring	12
Cardinals Nesting	14
Flowers at Pascha	16
Snow Bike	18
Spring Scandal	19
Caribou Memory	20
Rain Boy	22
Northern Piano	23
Montreal Pantoum II	24

SUMMER

Sometimes We Are Not Alone	29
Birth of a Cloud	30
Miss Mitchell's Clouds	31
Saving the Lighthouse	34
Late for Dinner	36
Made and Un-Made	38
Moving a Washing Machine	41
Clothes Pins	42
Thirsty	44

SAN MIGUEL

San Miguel Pantoum	49
Spring Hammock	50
Almond Blossoms	51
Fanfare	52
San Miguel Montgolfier	53

LOVE

Corsair Raid	57
Lovers' Fall	58

Stars Awaken	60
In the Afternoon	61
Reasons	62
His Eyes	64
Earthquake Coverage	65

FAMILY

Rise Up Daughter	69
Life Preserved	72
Villanelle for Old Age	74
Garden of the Dead	75
Perfect Order	78
ABOUT THE AUTHOR	83

Acknowledgments

Fond memories and sincere thanks to my parents, Betty and Patrick Alban and to "teacher my teacher", Judyth Hill.

dedicated to all who dare

to see and to speak

Northern Compass

Montreal

SEDUCTION

May day, gray day
cold day, old day of dreams
Spring day, ring day
of the bell to begin day, of taking out the trash-bin
of shedding the snakeskin
of cleaning out the cupboard, standing on the diving board
of plunging into this
poetry day, writing day
fighting day, fighting with laziness, with stress, with excess
with trying to impress
the reader.
Is the reader the writer?
The fighter, the biter
the biter bitten, smitten, frostbitten,
unwritten with the delete button
and the buttonhole, the keyhole, the porthole?
Ready for the button? Don't push it. Stroke it
and look, a surprise!
A woman to sympathize, energize, capsize,
to recognize and fantasize
and at last, to burst into a swarm of dragonflies
before your tired eyes.

Don't Look for Logic Here

Don't look for it in migrating butterflies
or in a sunset that wraps around the whole sky.
Don't look for logic in a roof-top hammock
that swings in the to-and-fro of tides.

Where's the sense in an orange tree offering fruit
and sweet blossom
on the same day?

Understand, if you can, the sublime beauty of an ugly person,
 the cry of a rooster at two in the morning.
Is there logic in liquid glass cooled and offering you liquid?
Quiet logic, modest and in her place, sober,
comforting and hemmed in.
But don't seek her here.

Let the wrong bus take you away.
Let the young waiter bring you a dish you never ordered
and bless him for his confusion.
Your hand will fall upon another book than
the one you sought.
Take it up.
Run from the lover you think will fulfill every desire.
Hide in the brush like a fox or flit around like a tiny finch.

Don't try to tame every mystery or allow poor logic
to have her hand
firm on the tiller.

In not searching everything will come
shy and retiring as a nightingale,
yet with a sweet song that knows nothing of logic
but everything of order, of eternity, of logic-baffled melody.

Montreal Pantoum I

My island city bathed in the river's wet embrace
Her bridges strands of a silver web span shore to shore
A dormered house, a balcony, a curved staircase
Come, stroll along marshy banks where rapids roar

Her bridges strands of a silver web span shore to shore
Sweltering summer then brilliant leaves of autumn fall to bless
Come stroll along marshy banks where rapids roar
Hear the hum of commerce, traffic and excess

Sweltering summers then brilliant leaves of autumn fall to bless
The empty churches, spires that decorate the town
Hear the hum of commerce, traffic and excess
Short triumph of the blizzard and the plow's soft growl

The empty churches, spires that decorate the town
Sidewalk cafes sacred to *l' apero, le flirt*
Short triumph of the blizzard and the plow's soft growl
Sweet spring of lilac, gangsters and *le cirque*

Sidewalk cafes sacred to *l'apero, le flirt*
A dormered house, a balcony a curved staircase
Sweet spring of lilac, gangsters and *le cirque*
My island city bathed in the river's wet embrace

Painters's Sky

Sometimes early in the winter morning the cold sky is just as he saw it. Clouds, grey and white or pink, pearly with early sun framed with winter trees, like besom brooms or fir trees or twisted twigs, black against the miracle morning sky.

The untouched blue that will change, deepen with the light of day. Just as he saw it.

How he stood in his heavy woolen coat trimmed with bear or beaver, his feet in good moccasins fashioned by some Kanawake woman, a fur cap to save his ears from the roaring wind.

How he stood to look, to remember moving clouds, the piled snow, the native, the trapper, the basket woman and the *habitant*. Far from his Dutch still-life studies. Here he stood to remember and render this sky.

Here were pictures to sell to British soldiers or to the landed French. Ah, did you know, Cornelius that your cold Quebec skies keep company now in old Beaverbrook's Museum with Constable, with Gainsborough and with Dali? No care for that now, the wind cutting this early pearly-sky morning. I stand where he stood, under the Kreighoff sky.

Path to Morning

Montreal awakens to a December morning.
The little city garden, steadfast, gallant, waiting
for a glance of admiration, of homage.
A lamp-post presides over the lane
welcoming birds and the old cat emperor.

Unable to resist that first step onto the back veranda,
happy surprise of sinking down,
my boot calls forth a soft wet groan
descending into the new kingdom.

Bushes and trees, the fence crowned and erect
hold their elegant curves.
Day comes on fast against retreating night.
Wind tugs at the perfect symmetry
traced on the lacy fence.
The lilac tosses off her pale jewels
in the hemmed –in garden.

Only I and the black emperor
will break the white seal this morning.
Beside the door the snow shovel stands
untouched until noon.

Cold Bronze

It is a little hard to stand witness
over the follies of the city.

Season after season they come
to admire us or to joke at our grave gaze.
The museum guides revere us and show us off
on lunchtime sculpture-garden tours.

In the heat of summer, our surfaces searing
under blazing sun
we hear again and again
who made us and how, and why.

In winter we contract into our sober images.

The crowd trundles by, eyes on the street.
Small tentative steps crunch down the hill.
A breathless slither over an ice patch camouflaged
with a dusting of snow.
No dreams now of bronze monuments
but rather of the cold need to stay upright.

Tired Love

Once the city welcomed Winter with his frost-art
on the kitchen window,
his soft jewel snowflakes fallen on a dark sleeve.
The power in his breath set bare branches clashing
in a harsh percussion.

But we are fickle and now we search
at street corners for the green-haired boy,
his cap trimmed with a bright feather.

Spring, you are late! Where are you hiding?
I return again and again to the window as if
waiting for a guest who promised to come,
or for a beloved child who forgets,
careless over his game, careless of my longing.

Late Spring, are you racing
down the great river that holds the island city captive
all the long bitter winter?
Sweep down with those great floes of ice that speed along
over the still untamed rapids.

Don't you hear the song of poor birds, your heralds
sitting high at the tops of leafless trees
to catch the first rays of sun?
Only when your soft breath
has whispered secrets to a sleeping lilac
can they nest.

Come, we promise to prune the vine
and to sit out on the porch at noon.
We promise to drink tea outdoors, carefully
placing chairs in the sun.
We promise to hang washing on the line
to praise snowdrops and crocuses
who dare in the little sheltered garden
to hear your singing voice.

Only come and set us free from him.
Caress our hands and faces with kisses soft or rough.
You are late, but come at last and in one warm day
we will forgive your late-coming!

Hard Spring

Spring in Montreal
is a breech birth.
We can feel it coming.
We can feel the earth groaning,
absorbing the ice and snow
of months of frigid darkness.

The sun, its warmth
no longer faint, fickle, theoretical,
coaxes, wheedles the first snowdrops, crocuses.
Those are never picked.

Now come the shoots of daffodils and tulips
and grass, that universal miracle
appears.

The sound of hardy birds, but still not a leaf.
A few closed buds along a twig
and heavy rain – the waters breaking
cold and painful.

The brave yellow blooms
stand against a meager unkind frost one night
and then, sap drips from a vine
and the whole city knows
a long warm day
with magnolias, pink or white like waxy cups or earth
stars opening on the leafless branches.

The moon rises soft and silvery
over the city blessed by newborn Spring.

Cardinals Nesting

Christmas card cliché – I never liked the predatory beak,
the fierce air
but for the first spring I have cardinals around me.
Perched in a tree just outside my garden, they search
for cover.
Leaf growth late this year, the pair flit back and forth.

I love robin song,
clear, fluting, a deep yearning note
familiar as the hand of
a lover, on my neck.

The well-known homely thrill repeated
every April to usher me out of the long grey winter.
But now, this pair,
the male brilliant, his fearless flight
mocking the feral cats.

And she, more discrete, and yet, her presence
more intense, more of life, eternity.
He sat yesterday on the edge
of an old bird bath I set up,
drinking his fill on the very first day of this supply of water.

Then at evening, the song
three loud clear notes repeated– sol – I found it
as I hummed the scale
and a burst of frilly trills
bubbling, choking notes, rich and full,
a long coloratura aria filling the neighborhood.
The workman, his hammer stilled raised his head to listen,
transfixed by song.

Flowers at Pascha

At a side altar, the Golgotha
Mary, her veil at her eyes
and John, head bowed
the beloved Christ and the sun and moon dismayed.

A woman approached with a glass vase
of spring flowers.
Tulips, lipstick red, orange and sun yellow
their hearts dark, black and golden stamens
and the thick fleshy leaves
standing up among the blooms.

The orange tulips hung down over the lip
of the vase, a prostration
their petals sharp and pointed.
The water was cool and transparent
for stems green and slender.
She brought in a vase of light, of air, of freshness.
She brought in a vase of courage, of joy, of tragedy
and brokenness.

They blazed and called out to the faithful
to look, to revel in the beauty of the world.
She placed them between two sober pots
that held twin orchids, white, angelic blooms.

They stood guard, their white faces flat and open.
Large and round, suspended on curved stems
and dark shield-like leaves, close to the pots.

The orchids pure, like meditative souls, bowed
to their worldly sisters.
Those grave angels, their hearts lightened by the fire of tulips.

Snow Bike

Speeding along in summer and in the breezy haze
of autumn colors, golden leaves flung up
by your spinning wheels.
Did you dream, in a shredded-feather dream
of your snow-fixed immobility on this
street-light lit night?

I think not. I think you flew along in the Zen moment
Of rolling the kilometers under your two wheels.
And now your two wheels are under.

Speed turned to solid
Light turned to lead
Sprite turned to statue
Your elegant skeleton outlined in thick white weight.
This too a Zen moment, something you did not expect
but made for you, snow bike.

Spring Scandal

Tulips red as a whore's lipstick.
Red like a cheap plastic toy,
as strawberry Kool-aid.
Yellow as colored margarine,
a kid's bathing suit
a can't-look-at-me sun.

Sexy pistils stand up in black-hearted cups.
Pushy cups seduce innocent bees and tiny wasps.
The fleshy tulip leaves, mild green, are aghast at
the showy goblets
sprung up among them.

Prim gardener, showing off your cheeky beauties,
your garden porn!

Caribou Memory

Under the huge sky, the gusty wind as my companion
I came upon your remains.
The others, far off and picking berries, had no idea
of the few moments we spent together.
I thought of the day you were left behind as the great herd
thundered away past the town.
Even your mother, caught up in the thud
of hooves, the drum drive
to cover miles and miles that day
did not miss you or search
over the wide tundra, dotted here and there with poor trees.

You fell to your knees, weak or lame and as you fell
with one eye you saw the great sky.
Silence soon came and then night, and cold.
You slept a little, stiffening. As the moon set
you saw the stars
dim and fade.
The sun rose and with it a little pale comfort.
Your breath that day stirred the tiny leaves of plants
low to the ground.
You breathed out your spirit onto the tundra and a gust of
wind welcomed you
into infinity.

A few years later I came upon your skull,
the faint blush of blood still in your antlers.
Your jaw, sea green, a skim of moss shadowing the bone.
Alone, alone in the wind, under the great sky,

I bent to take you, take you home.
In truth, you were home, but I took you still
as a trophy to loneliness.

Rain Boy

The red-headed boy and his mother
run in the morning of rain.
Run as all red-headed boys before him.
Running in Ireland, Scotland, in Norway.
Running away from, running toward
the steady cool rain,
A thatch of thick straight red hair to run
off the steady cool rain.
The rain and the red-headed boy and his mother
running and laughing, running to summer.
Rain, run to the river.
Boy, run from the giver of life, your mother.
A summer of rain and the red-headed boy.
The trees and I stand
and smile at the running of rain and the red-headed boy.

Northern Piano

Even here, a sound
silvery and brave and don't-care beautiful.
Complex and perfect
easy and arrogant.
Above the blowing grit,
above the grey river, the bar,
above the stray dogs and the rough grass.
In these notes are Warsawa and Krakow.
In the little flat today are the spires, the Baltic,
the uncut forest, palaces and snow-capped Carpathians,
Chopin in unsuspecting Kuujjuaq.

Montreal Pantoum II

Janus, god of the port and of beginnings, smiles on our Montreal
Home to every hue and creed
Home to a hundred tongues, our brash French drawl
We come to succeed, to fail, to follow or to lead

Home to every hue and creed
Mohawk and French, the English, now the world
We come to succeed, to fail, to follow or to lead
Today at the airport stands a frightened girl

Mohawk and French, the English, now the world
To this mosaic each one some bright tesserae will bring
Today at the airport stands a frightened girl
Step forward now and will your new life to begin

To this mosaic each one some bright tesserae will bring
Sing a strong song, a poem, hold out your woven shining strand
Step forward now and will your new life to begin
Though in your heart you carry your homeland

Sing a strong song, a poem, hold out your woven shining strand
Home to a hundred tongues, our brash French drawl
Though in your heart you carry your homeland
Janus god of the port and of beginnings smiles on our Montreal

Summer

Sometimes We Are Not Alone

In the dark night as I lay sleeping
in the low mist of no-dreaming sleep,
a spirit, a little soul came.

There, I can hear you snorting, harrumphing,
"Ridiculous, why not just say a moth?"
It was a moth but so light, fluttering, seeking,
looking for a little water.
There was a little water. How prudent,
how prudent to put a glass of water beside my bed.
Yes, I laughed too to imagine myself taking a good long
swallow of water and moth in the middle of the night.
Down, down, like Jonah he would go.
No three day reprieve here.
That would have been the end of him.

In the morning when I made my bed and picked up
the cool glass of water
I looked to see a sign of life and quickly, quickly before I
could make up my mind threw the water out into the bushes
in hopes that he would fly.

There, now do you see why I called him a little soul?

Birth of a Cloud

The first time I saw a cloud born
it rose up out of a deep narrow valley.

It was springtime in a hot dry country that would
soon consume the moisture of its small rare forests.
It was a cool evening during Easter week.
I was out walking with someone whose name
is now forgotten.

We stood watching the mist rise up from the stream,
from the small trees clinging to the sides of the ravine.
It broke free of earth, lifting and drifting.
I understood at that moment how clouds are born.
I understood that the cloud could dissipate in fierce sun
or mass with other clouds and rain somewhere close
or far away.

I thought about mighty oceans and storm clouds.
I grasped the idea that the drop falling from a tropical leaf
or shaken from the feather of a bird,
was water I might drink one day, or use to rinse a cloth.
Water in a great plantation, harnessed to irrigate a crop,
water I would shed in tears. All one water,
All Ganges water, all Nile water, all Jordan water,
all Amazon water.

Bow to the cloud as it is born then. Bow and do not forget
the birth of clouds.

Miss Mitchell's Clouds

Clouds from both sides now
oh, Joni, both sides, both sides?
Just the two sides you mean?

Huge white hills over there
around and behind my head
as far, farther than the horizon.
Needle sharp shards on a pale blue
winter sky – standing upright –
blown upright by the bitter wind.

Layers of softest grey and gold
at sunset.
Storm clouds that terrify
great purple masses – grumbling
into thin sickly yellow linings.

Or a tunnel cloud
touching down to destroy,
to shatter with a feather touch.
Night clouds, pale and indistinct
against the navy blue sky.
A sky full of infinite possibilities,
benign and sheltering
decorated here and there with the unreal clouds.

Dull grey snow clouds
hanging over the city
waiting and waiting for the wind

to blow and tear them open
waiting to release their heavy load of snowflakes
to silence the great city
to smooth out the lanes and fence posts
to make the lovers see that their prickly little quarrels
cannot stand under the winter clouds and their cold cargo.

A cloud forming in the deep gorge lined with a silver stream.
The mist rising at evening
gathering moisture from the pine trees
under the eye of the old dog, of the tired shepherd
rising and freeing itself at last
from the ties of earth to sport in the sky
at the mercy of the breezes of night. A little cloud.

Ah Miss Mitchell, both sides, both sides?
Have you looked from both sides? Have you made a song
from both sides?
Ah, Miss Mitchell, look at the rolling little earth
spinning in the thrall of the little burning sun.
Look, Miss Mitchell at the circle of the horizon.
Look, Miss Mitchell at the flat disk of the moon
slipping beneath the clouds.
Such thousands, such thousands of miles
between the poor vapors
and the cold clay
that tricks us with the stolen light of her brother sun.
And love. The beating heart, almost round but not quite.
Such anguish and such joy that lifts the lovers
off their feet as Chagall shows us.
Swept above the kind earth by their love if only for a moment.
A lover's love.
A mother's love that without question gives.

A father's love silent and torn, dumb before the little child.
The hand of a friend held in warm smooth companionship,
the patient and the doctor, the teacher and the pupil,
the clement judge and the prisoner in the dock.
The green eye of the cat on a cold night when all
is snug at home
or of the dog as his leash is clipped on.
The look in the eye of a stranger on the subway.
Well, look at love then.

And the round year, Miss Mitchell, what of that?
Spinning and turning and folding in upon itself.
The little round bush outside my window
exposed as a ball of twigs under the snow clouds
decorated with frost.
And turning, turning into the green and verdant
spring herald of rebirth. The resurrection lilac
and the mother of life in summer, her belly round
with tiny seeds, profligate, excessive, resplendent with life
and agony of death – the round little tree, brown
or gold or red as blood.
Dying to live and coming alive again and again.
Miss Mitchell, look from both sides, by all means.
To look around is to fall on my face in wonder and
adoration of clouds.

Saving the Lighthouse

Set on the windy highland where blasted trees
struggle for survival.
By definition prey to storms.
No silence here, the breath of wind and shush of wave below
punctuated by the cries of gulls,
sighing wet breath of humpback or minke whales.
And from time to time the chugging motor of a fishing boat.

The lighthouse.
Saved, restored, shored up, paid up,
cabled up, held up, kept erect, alive.
But wait, isn't that your job, lighthouse?
Standing up in all weathers, in all winds,
eternally saving, restoring to the shore some puny mortal?
Of course, now there's radar and sonar, GPS I suppose, but
still, there's something forever about a lighthouse.

I used to lie down here in the summer grass where wild roses
spread over the windy peninsula.
I'd wake to bees or crickets and follow
the paths of desire over the rough ground.
I never dreamed a lighthouse would need help.

For decades in the sunny days the keeper's wife would knit
or nurse her child. In the winter nights the light, the bell,
sometimes the deep fog horn would sound.And those at sea
would chart and steer a course, safe in that way at least.

The keeper tending the light in the high wind-shuddering
lantern, peering into snow or darkness.
He knew he and the light had done the best, the best
they could.

Long gone the lighthouse keeper and his wife,
long gone the many wrecks.
So must we save the lighthouse?
Is there "forever" on this rocky wreck-strewn coast?

Late for Dinner

What is this place where they tell you they'll wait
dinner for you
because there are right whales off the lighthouse?
You have a little time and maybe you'll see them.
What is this place where the broad flat sea stretches away
from the lace-rimmed rocks,
out to the horizon where the pale sky sits?

The swallow-tail light is as white as a virtuous woman.
The air rivals the wine left half-drunk in the glass.
I push back my chair and go out where the sea birds
are clustered together
in tremulous knowledge of the two right whales.

They are there and sometimes I can see their plumes,
white against the blue sea far off out from shore.
I wait patiently in the early evening, the breeze waiting too,
gentle on my light-clad arms.
I would be glad, no, transported with joy to see them
although they might not breach, might not show a fin or tail.

Even in this place I cannot wait until dark.
I cannot keep the others waiting. The others
are of my kind and
wondering where I can be.

Even though I can only feel the great ones there off shore,
and know as sure as sure
that they are there. Well, that is enough

and more than enough
to transport me to the watery depths,
to the cold boundless places where the right whales
with no regard for me, attend to their right business.

What is this place where no bird, nor seal, nor tree,
nor breeze, nor wave,
pays any attention to my tender waiting?
It is the right place.

Made and Un-Made

Cars and houses and even an asphalt
street rolling on up that hill,
wonders, real wonders for human beings
a whole world to fill.
Fashioning the world, drawn out, drawn, spun out
to some fantastic peak
of art, of technology, of skill
of stubborn persistence, of flawless technique.

Trial and error, over and over again
rewarded by money, power and fame
by prestige, vanity and real interest too.
The fullness of heart and intellect
that knows the triumph of doing it, getting it, knowing it
through and through.
Knowing that you can, that you do it
better than anyone else.

Yes, Mr. Einstein, Mr. Edison, Mr. Faberge,
Yes, cowboy, or doctor or builder of a great railway.

One who was called, "teacher, my teacher,"
by a student who got it, in whose eyes light dawned.
The acrobat, the soccer player, the toolmaker,
or are tools now made by laser?
A toolmaker as obsolete as an emperor.

But trees, no – trees live apart from us
beside, parallel, apart from the asphalt street

from the wrist watch, the iPad, the latest sneakers
on the feet that walk the asphalt street.

Yes, clouds and trees
look – a dark form, the early summer leaves.
Oh, is it sun or rain or time that weaves
the formed dark silhouette or filigree pattern of the twigs
stenciled against the pale clouds?

Within the dark form, the trunk and branches
there creatures live, birds or squirrels, insects
unobserved even at early morning
when the red-headed boy runs in the rain
that falls on the asphalt and down the city drain.
The rain that falls into the river
on my red car or onto the muddy lane.

Come then, rain and wind. Come clouds, come snow.
Grow grass and trees, weeds, bushes, come seasons' flow.
Fly birds, annoy me squirrels and mosquitoes and flies.
Charm me, butterflies and dragonflies and bees and wasps
tight laced. Live your lives, damn it.

Insist, as we insist on some crazy object.
Arise moon behind the clouds. Be perfect.
As perfect as a Faberge egg? Let's troop to see that.
Let's pay to see it, study it, marvel at it, guard it
photograph it, explain it. Let's just get it, shall we?
Do you get it? Well, then, let's lose it.

Let's pick a leaf from some ragged lilac bush
Let's stand and look at that dark shape.
An egg, a tree. Where are we?

Moving a Washing Machine

Today the grave and muscled young mover
comes with someone else.
Chantal, she of sinewy calves and arms, the black hair
and ice-blue eyes, the lady mover,
the womanly mover, with her coaxing, managing spirit,
eyeing the narrow door, the steep steps.

Chantal of the dangerous smile, not at all dismayed
at the task,
laughing, calling for tools to dismantle, to reassemble
the bulky matter
that is, after all, necessary for the laundress, the housewife.

No hurry or ego here, just the belt and a look between her
and the grave, muscled young man.
Midwife to a washing machine, slipped through
the impossibly narrow doorway.

I bow to muscles, manipulation, the mastery
of the material world.
Honest payment, quick and no bargaining, a tip,
a beer and then
the manipulator of the material world kisses me
on both cheeks
and to my smiling astonishment backs the moving van
gently into the fence.
A treacherous realm, the material world.

Clothes Pins

Wet clothes hung on the line
in brilliant sunshine.
Shirt sleeves reach out over the flower bed.
Crayon-colored tulips, crimson and dandelion yellow
jostle in a slight breeze.
The old blue scarf, pinned at the edges
bellies out, a ship's sail on a time voyage.
Talisman against the eye on so many first meetings,
or ominous family get-togethers.
Blue charm of softness, my ally.

White facecloths, tidy squares, bleached
purified under the burning sun.
Dipped in cold water
they've wiped a face hot with tears,
other hot parts too, wet with sweat or love.
White facecloths, humble and chastened,
woven witnesses, silent and patient.

Reel in that line and send out white sheets
folded width-wise to stop them catching
on the thorny rose bush.
Lift gently, flutter and swoop down, settle down.
Pillow cases embroidered with red hearts and green tendrils
old tears long washed away in the soapy chug chug
of the machine.
New ones to come from that human spring that can never be
stopped up, blocked up, paved over.
Always swelling up with old griefs, or new.

Bed clothes, tell your tales now to the wind,
Tales of a thousand and one nights. More than that!
Lucky Scheherazade who always had an audience.
Lucky Penelope who unraveled her cares, her hopes by night.

Tell my tales, years of secret ecstacy, of loneliness, betrayal
and of most pernicious hope.
Sleepless nights you witnessed, the night-born worries
creeping up onto the bed and down between
my body and the top sheet.

Or, at last, the soft turn to the right, pillow just so, beneath
the cheek and chin.
Dreams that only you in the still darkness
soak up and keep until
stripped from the mattress and stuffed into the old machine
you find relief from these wounds, these transports,
flushed out on the second rinse cycle.

Hang still for a few moments
in the strong morning sunlight.
Moisture leaching out into the eager air.
Kind companions of all I bring to you at night.
Myself, another, dreams or tears. Only to you do I entrust
my river, my galaxy, my tide.

Thirsty

So thirsty,
the good feel of water
gulped down thoughtlessly from a bottle.
Water renewing a tired body, seeping into blood and cell,
flowing through the little universe.

Washing with scented soap and rinsing.
The flow of saliva at the smell of soup.
Steam from the little red kettle calling for the cup of tea.
A kiss, the taste of that mouth, misty breath mingled
with mine, sweet wet longing
of desire and bodies dewy with sweat.

Rain on the window, driven to ice on the twigs and leaves.
Ice on the mountain top melting slowly and feeding a stream,
a broad river pushing on to the sea.
The saltiness of it, varying tides,
  towering waves that rise in some far place beyond imagining.
They strike cold the heart of the captain,
the crew, for there is no escape.
The following day, blue and benign, calm and vast
with only a swell to beguile, to soothe,
to wipe away that terror.
Fine spray cast aside by the great vessel
and the straight wake.

Irrigation channels reviving parched fields.
Wells, deep and cool where magic frogs or monsters live,
where the butter is kept,
where trysts are kept, where brave souls descend
to enter, alive, the underworld.

Swamps where earth and water mate, breed, mingle together
and all nature flocks
and teems as nowhere else.
The polar caps, besieged as they are,
retreating glaciers, disappearing seas

Water flowing through us day by day
when we are tender fields,
terraced hills put to hard work,
rocky canyons worn away.
Until the very last drink of water and then we come
to other elements,
fire or earth.

San Miguel

San Miguel Pantoum

San Miguel evening, sunset and a star.
Small pomegranate flowers, lipstick red
round jewels, a bell rings from afar
a chance, a whim, I am led.

Small pomegranate flowers, lipstick red
glimpsed above a blue wall.
A chance, a whim, I am led.
A woman sits at the street corner.

Glimpsed above a blue wall
small jewels shining in green leaves.
A woman sits at the street corner
among rough cobble-stones.

Small jewels shining in green leaves
I wander lost in narrow streets
among rough cobble stones
after the heat of a winter day.

I wander lost in narrow streets
round jewels, a bell rings from afar
after the heat of a winter day
San Miguel evening, sunset and a star.

Spring Hammock

Swinging in the spring hammock
under the late evening sky.

The stars come out.

Up on the roof terrace with its yellow flowers
and the brilliant sky darkening down
I hear the faint creak of the star-burst twined ropes.

One bright star above rocks with me so that I am not lonely.
Hold me in your arms rocking hammock.
Gaudy pink geraniums fluorescent against
the salmon colored wall
keep me company.

And the shadow of the splayed ropes against the cooling wall.

Back and forth, creak, creak.
The two-note bell
from the parish church
calls my heedless rocking soul to repentance.

Almond Blossoms
after a Greek folk song

Almond tree with your dark slender boughs,
like an ardent lover
you put forth your blossoms.

You dare to decorate your twigs with small flowers,
white or pink, pure, clustered along the black branches.

Like an ardent lover
you take the risk
before your leaves have formed,
before the sun has coaxed forth the green mist
of spring leaves,
before frost is surely vanquished and driven out.

At night you tremble
like an ardent lover in the cold.
Risk taker, reckless of the tender blooms
yet prudent in your gamble.

At every spring sight of a blossoming almond,
I remember how I stood beneath the little tree
on a square of waste ground in Athens
and heard the thrum, the throb of life
as tiny wasps and bees, hungry and eager for the first blooms
ravished you and consummated your love,
ardent lover.

Fanfare

All the bright day
the half moon hangs pale in the sky.
Now, at evening, as I rock in the hammock
she gains in luster.
Swing, green hammock!
Hide her and reveal her
behind terra-cotta roof tiles.
A pale ribbon of frothy cloud
comes as welcome,
to veil her as blue dusk
ushers her out
to sit
on her dark throne.

San Miguel Montgolfier

Bombastic balloon beribbed with colors,
gassy and veering over the town
peering into secret enclosed gardens where
rooted and grounded trees hung with spheres
orange or green or pomegranate vermillion
sway and bob in the early breeze.

The morning air is a little too *movemente*
for safety, yet daring balloonist, you light your great flame
and roar and rise and billow out fabric.

There it goes bellying up over the basket
above the hidden orchard town.

The little pomegranates, hardly out of skirts yet
bow and curtsey and glitter in the green leaves.
They attend effortlessly to their business of chambers
of red juice, like crimson honey combs sweet and sticky.
The exhilarated triumphant balloonist deflates, coasts
and bumps to earth.
A tiny pomegranate falls from a tree and rolls away.

Love

Corsair Raid

Pirate eyes, black and difficult to read,
deep set, shaded by bushy eyebrows.
A raider, a marauder, bringing with you the scent
of wide-open sea.
Without permission, without leave
you bent, awkward but sure
to imprint a salty kiss
that tasted faintly of scotch and almonds.
No words.
I heard the snap of a sail driven by a west wind
the rush of sea water.
Down, down
eight bells.

Lovers' Fall

After a dry hot autumn where the only moisture
was the salty tears streaming unbidden from my eyes,
the days became shorter, light withdrew
in the muddled metro cars full of absent people.

Tears spilled at the sight of shoes like yours
or a book you liked to read clutched in another's hand.
All the sights of the water-bound city were as dust to me.
The round green mountain a heap of stones bereft of charm.
My joints creaked and moaned as they must
move along familiar streets,
the sky others praised as brilliant, dull and harsh.
The golden leaves a dead chore.
And then, one day, a rainy day, the first for a long time
you came, impatient to the door
and with a few words we prepared food.
Dark beer for a toast. A toast! Was it possible?

After the food and drink
the bed,
that poor bed, how dull and dark it had grown,
a repository of cries, of clouded eyes.
That day it became a white cloud
a bedecked steed
a flurry of snowflakes
a white hot flame
a bird's soft plumage
fragrant white lilies of the dark garden

white jasmine and snowdrops
narcissus fragrant and tuberose
homely white geranium with dark green leaves.

The sealed white parchment with its red wax was
at last opened
the red wine and white bread of our holy communion.
But make no mistake, here were bodies
the warm hands, lips wet and longing for the other
and for the breast
those hands, so dear – at last, at last
and both solicitous for the other's pleasure and joy
bringing forth our own blessed stream and flow,
and at last fatigue and quiet
the breath of the beloved, that sweetest sound.

And both of us a little asleep
and a little awake
resting, resting at last from a dry autumn
as the blessed rain and wind beat upon the dark window.

Stars Awaken

On the darkest day
on the cloudy November day
when we turn the hands
of the watch, of the clock,
when we wring our hands
to wring from the short day
a little light,
on that short dark day
see the stars, the stars of scintillating, sparkling,
spangling light
shine in you.

Diamonds waiting in you to blaze and blink
to dazzle and blind
with joy
lighting the stars in me
the touch of your calm hand on mine.

See how the tree, the little bush
blazes up with starlight
its last leaves kindled, radiant.
Endless starlight bursts forth from its leaves.
And from my smile, my eyes
from my hand warmed by your hand.

So shine out then with diamonds, stars, gems, spangles
shine as does the little tree
a touch of your hand – my stars awaken

In the Afternoon

Sleep surged over you like a bore tide
we had once seen run fast up river.
The bend of your legs vulnerable, like that of a child's
under the green blanket.
Your white hair sunk into the pillow,
soberly trimmed with a narrow band of crochet,
surf along the dark rock of your profile.

Sleep breaths, heavy with fatigue, precious every one.
I heard them, watched them rise and fall, soft sea swells.

Your face was stern in the dark land.
The self in another dreaming or dreamless place.
Eyes shuttered to any quick glance,
less mysterious than your waking face.
Such a vanquished air.
Spears thrown down at the gate of the sea-side fortress,
drunk guards asleep.

Reasons

Not you – it's me
love absentee
his PhD
and family tree
something for free
a Christmas tree
he sang off-key
that . . . . . Ann Marie!
A gambling spree
too fancy free
no referee
well, pardon me
but in reality
it's fear that broke us up
for though we're so grown up
to really open up
needs courage, heaven sent
for an engagement truly meant
a neck that's bent
bent to the other's heart
a plunge, trust, a leap
into unknown so deep
that some prefer to keep
their love well locked away
safe, out of danger, no real need to say
the words

to break the seal
of fear
and in that way
we touch antennae
and creep soft away.

His Eyes
from a line by W.B. Yeats

Cold as the March wind, his eyes
Chilled by sights of death and sorrow.
Trained up from youth for command
Stern as the winter blast, his voice.

Softened to a May breeze, his whisper
When seldom, oh so seldom
Love runs ahead in the race of work or care
Love, as a game, a toy, a plaything.

Warm as September sunshine, his embrace
Brief and bereft of hope.
Take it in the few afternoon hours
that he allots for this relief.

Ever absorbed in struggle and in striving
His heart set upon the prize
Hold for a moment, rough with work, his hand
Cold as the March wind, his eyes.

Earthquake Coverage

Twenty years ago the dishes rattled
in the kitchen cupboard.
Standing on a chair to choose the cups
to take to my
break-up, heartbreak, tear-flood flat,
I felt the chair shake, heard the plates chatter
and believed my grief
had made an earthquake.

No longer the centre of the universe,
answering the insurance agent's odd but vital questions.
A poured concrete basement, a tar and gravel roof,
Extra earthquake coverage?
This is Quebec, not L.A. or Haiti, not Nepal or Vancouver
So, perhaps not. The cups are silent in this house
and besides, I never remarried.

Family

Rise Up Daughter

So much suspense surrounds the making of bread.
So many theories, certainties, so much advice.
One way, one secret, one wish
will make it perfect
this time.

Magic yeast, secret and commonplace
there in its paper envelope on the shelf in the market
decade after decade.
There is only one brand of yeast.

Careful, check the date on the package!
Even the eternal yeast maker
might ship out an old batch, a dead batch.
No, it's new, well before its due date.
Although a due date is for birth, not death.

My yeast is eager to munch up sugar,
loll around in warm milk,
froth up like some fresh teenage Cleopatra
giving herself to the "creative process."
She fizzes up the beginning of the whole affair
flirty, flaunting her musky, beery smell.
She holds the baker ransom to her
popping, swelling lively growth.

"Thank God. That's OK. Now for the flour."
Sifting into the bowl in a slap-dash way
not used to this business

in the take-out, bang, crash kitchen
with my lined yellow pad and my lap-top
perched up on top of the fridge.
Out of the way on bread-making day.

What the hell is all-spice?
A bit of cinnamon and nutmeg will have to do.
Froth up the eggs and sugar, can't go wrong.
Coddle that yeast, mind
not too hot and no draughts.
Seems that cheeky adolescent is delicate, fussy,
a real princess. Anything could kill her

Mix it all up and pray the phone doesn't ring
now that fingers are heavy, wet and stuck together.

And sort it out, woman!
Knead it, bash it on the wooden table.
Give it a good going over.
Knead for ten minutes the book said.
No wonder the old-tyme women
had good arms.

Damn! Started too late, didn't read the recipe right
Twice put to rise – twice!
No sleep this night.
Braid up the dough
traditional method – cobbled off You-Tube.
My mother's way? She was busy at holidays
with hats and cocktail parties to honor the hats.

Never mind, she'll eat this tomorrow.
She'll love it and shake her head
at my skill in this
and as she spreads the butter into the hot heart
of the bread I give her, she'll grieve that I never got
a good husband to enjoy this bread.
Better to have been skilled in the ways of hats
or golf, she'll say, that's where the men are!

Still much to do
before she sinks her poorly fitting teeth
into this loaf made for the Spring feast.
A warm place to sit to rise
and finally the baking, the dreamy smell of yeast
working away.
I must be sure not to fall asleep
and burn the bread.
Burnt offerings to the god of hats.

Next day, in the late afternoon
my daughter at the door
presents a golden loaf.
Perfection, braided high and light.

Another spring, Passover, Pascha, passing on
a love of sweet bread
a love of hats
love.

LIFE PRESERVED

My daughter brought me a bracelet of flat disks.
"They make bracelets out of some sort of nut in Hawaii."
The disks are green and smooth
as the curving waves
shot through with brown tangles,
sea weed or fish.
Indistinct, just glimpsed in the clear curve
of salt water tumbling through wonderlit mirrors.

My daughter said she stared at waves for hours.
She rode a few waves.
The struggle to paddle out, bent low to get into position
to ride.
Pushing against the swell and rush to shore,
she pulled out, panting behind the ride-waves.
Proud she could get out there but frightened
under the open-up sky
Thrill-girl
now in middle age, her arms aching and one
ankle injured, weak.

She knelt on the board
the way a kind older woman had shown her.
That woman had made a life of waves.
Not enough, never enough for Thrill-girl
to sit on the beach and watch willowy girls or sinewy boys
half her age sashay or swoop in to the beaten sand
on the creeping, rising, roaring, cresting, swooning,
crashing waves.

The green-brown disks of the bracelet
are drilled right through.
The elastic sits snug on my forearm, just above my right wrist.
Broken wrist with the ugly outer bone.

Sometimes a clear heavy wave
roars a little too close
and I taste salty water
in the back of my throat.
I blink the whole Pacific out of my
dazzled eyes – amazed at the endless, day-night relentless
little cruelties.

I trace with my left first finger a large flat disk.
"Some sort of Hawaiian nut."

Her competent hand
clasps steady around my arm, my wrist,
holding me at the tipping point
of the wave.

Villanelle for Old Age

I have learned to sit still.
They come and find me here
in my house on the hill.

The mailman brings a letter or a bill.
There is nothing left to fear.
I have learned to sit still.

I drink and eat my fill,
a slice of meat, a glass of beer,
in my house on the hill.

The nurse comes with a tonic or a pill.
I don't know why. She's never clear.
I have learned to sit still.

They tell me sign a cheque and make my will.
I can't quite see them. I can't hear.
In my house on the hill.

I want to laugh, to dance and cheer,
to kiss my love, but I am ill.
I have learned to sit still
in my house on the hill.

Garden of the Dead

I saw her last breath, the last tiny breeze
of many, many years exhaling out into the universe
a butterfly wing-beat in the garden world.

Palm Sunday, the first spring visit
to her grave.
I put some palms and pots of daffodils
and said "Hello".
I never pray there
in the safe and beautiful cemetery where foxes
and groundhogs
hide for the few moments that I visit.

In her last years she came to my garden
by the overgrown lane.
I'd drive her in the red car
and let her in at the little gate where she would stand still
for a few minutes
to see what was blooming, what was living there.
Then a few steps with the cane,
and again stopping for another look to see
what she had missed.

White lilies fit for Gabriel or pink peonies that came
from her own garden,
huge irises of palest blue or golden yellow. Big black-hearted

crimson poppies or violet morning glory and the grape vine
shading the table with its cool leaves.
She was right to stand and look.
How impatient I was then
sometimes dodging round her.
Why I wonder? What was there to do that was so vital?
But I must set a chair for her and bring a drink
and a soft cushion
for she was pitifully thin.

Still, her old and beautiful face
pulled like the moon, like a magnet, like an addiction
so that people would come and sit beside her
and look into that face.
My neighbor or a friend of mine. They'd come and pull
a chair beside her
as if she were some oracle or sage.
She was not wise but wisdom
resided in her face, in her grace, in her manner
imported from some other age.
When Filomena saw her from the next-door window she
would come in homage
with flowers in a posy or espresso coffee and her
cookies, just to chat
in her strange jargon of Italian and Quebec French
and even English , here and there
for "Madame Betty".
She might have said "Queen Betty" and been quite exact.

In her old age she claimed her queenly role and under her
large summer hat
she smiled indulgently on Filomena.
Queen Betty, deaf and ignorant of any language but her own
nodded graciously and replied in *non sequitors*,
as rulers often do.
She could charm any random stranger
who came into her court.

Now she has her own garden and a few
close-packed neighbors.
Unfortunate that they have none of Filomena's tact.
They do not leave when we are tired of them.
But I have seen the little rosebush bloom in summer,
coral blossoms and the box- wood shrubs
mark her domain. "Narrow, very narrow," she would say.
And I must stand above her to say, "Hello", as she lies
like a queen in state.

Perfect Order

Picked carelessly from the hedge
a stem that stood up above the rest.
I twirled it round as I stood watching for the yellow bus
that carries them by, so I can blow a kiss and wave
before the school day shadows them with its "behave".

And as I waited, listening for some bird or wondering
at a sea gull, a sea-way gull we'll say in Montreal,
I looked and saw the stem
with tiny rain beads, each a gem.

Leaves placed two by two
but one pair facing east-west and the other north-south,
safe in the bracket of the leaves, the flowers,
budding, blooming, fading, dropping off
in perfect order as they take their place
ascending on the stem in simple grace.

There they were, waving from the bus
claiming their place, their moment,
driving by so quickly, a small pale face,
a blossom at the window, the flutter of a hand,
ascending as I waved them on.

About the Author

Isobel Cunningham was born in Wales where she learned to love the songs in words. She has lived in Greece, in Poland and in the Canadian Arctic. Although she winters in magical San Miguel, Mexico, she is always glad to return to the city that inspires much of her writing, Montreal, Canada.

She is a docent at the Montreal Museum of Fine Arts, a devoted gardener and a writer of fiction and poetry. For interesting images and writing on a variety of topics, you are invited to visit her blog at *isobelmtl.wordpress.com*.

www.ingramcontent.com/pod-product-compliance
Lightning Source LLC
Chambersburg PA
CBHW031203090426
42736CB00009B/767